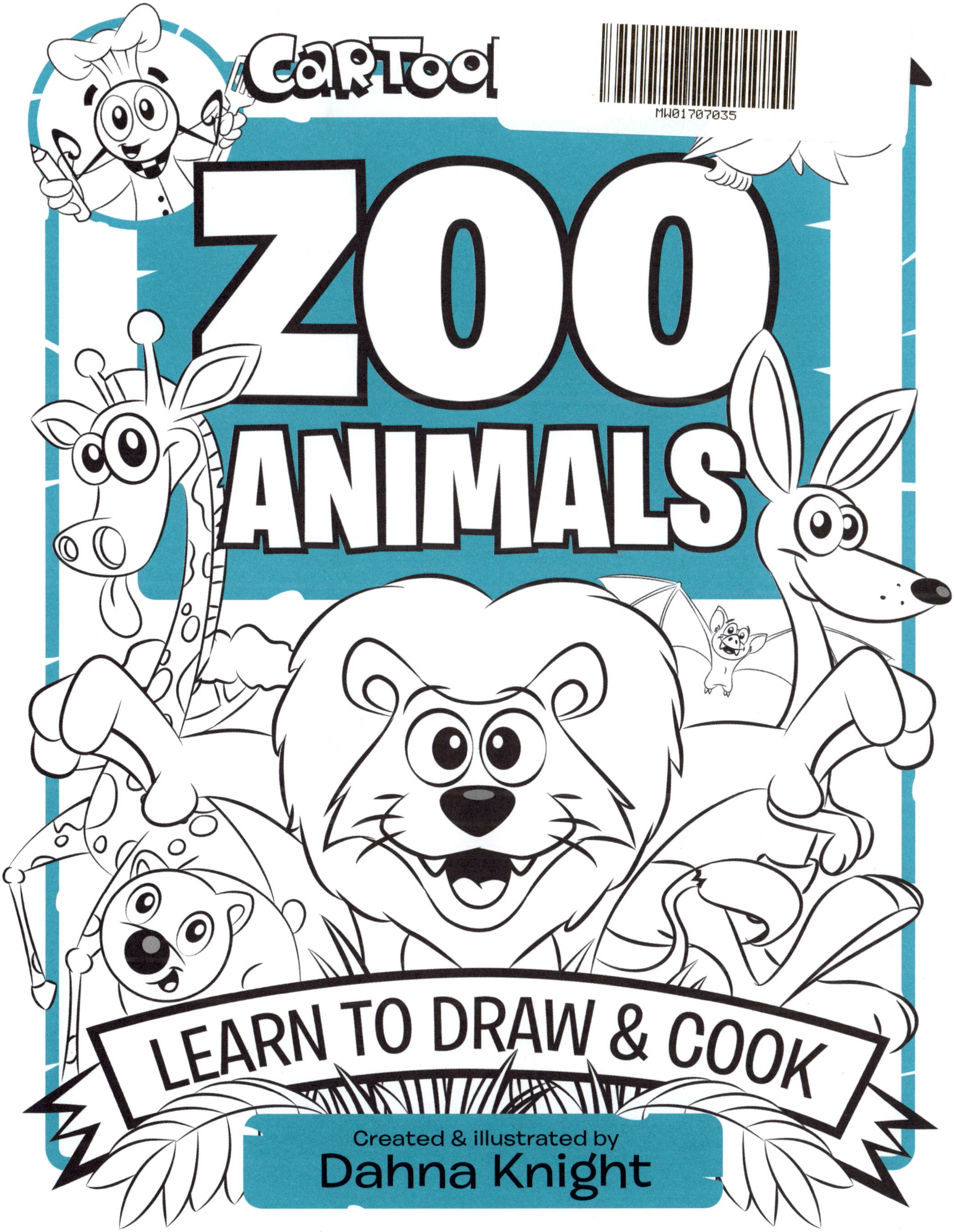

CarToo

ZOO ANIMALS

LEARN TO DRAW & COOK

Created & illustrated by
Dahna Knight

ChirpyBird

ChirpyBird

Cartoon Chef: Zoo Animals
published in 2013 by Chirpy Bird,
an imprint of Hardie Grant Egmont
Ground Floor, Building 1, 658 Church Street
Richmond, Victoria 3121, Australia

www.hardiegrantegmont.com.au

Introduction by Dahna Knight
Text by Chantal Gibbs
Design by Ash Oswald @ Hey There's Me

www.cartoonchef.com.au

Printed in China by Asia Pacific Offset

1 3 5 7 9 10 8 6 4 2

CONTENTS

SAFARI
RAINFOREST
OUTBACK
MARINE
BIRD SANCTUARY
CREEPY CRAWLIES

HELLO THERE,
LITTLE ARTISTS AND CHEFS!

IT IS TIME TO COOK UP A SCRUMPTIOUS FEAST OF CARTOONS AND RECIPES.

I am the

CARTOON CHEF,

here to teach you the ways of cartooning and cooking in easy-to-follow steps.

This book is going to take us on a tour of the wild and wacky wildlife found in the zoo. On our trip we will learn to draw many cute, cuddly, creepy and crazy creatures – and then cook a totally tasty recipe at the end of each chapter.

SO GRAB YOUR TRUSTY PENCILS, PAPER, SAUCEPANS, SPOONS AND SPATULAS, AND LET'S VISIT THE ZOO!

SAFARI

LION

HOW TO DRAW A LION

1.

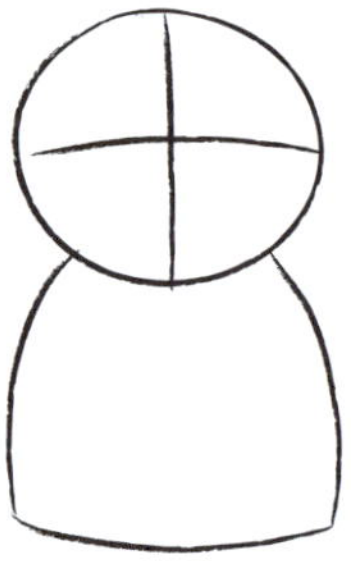

2.

3.

4.

5.

NOW IT'S YOUR TURN:

DID YOU KNOW?

This large cat's roar is so loud it can be heard from 8 kilometres away. Lions also like their rest and can laze around for 21 hours a day.

ELEPHANT

HOW TO DRAW AN ELEPHANT

1.

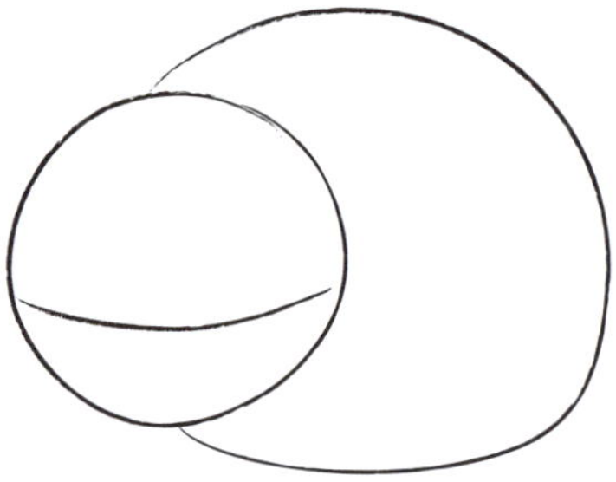

2.

3.

4.

5.

NOW IT'S YOUR TURN:

DID YOU KNOW?

An elephant's trunk is a specialised nose with more than 150,000 muscles, but no bones. Some elephants can actually draw and paint with their trunks!

GIRAFFE

HOW TO DRAW A GIRAFFE

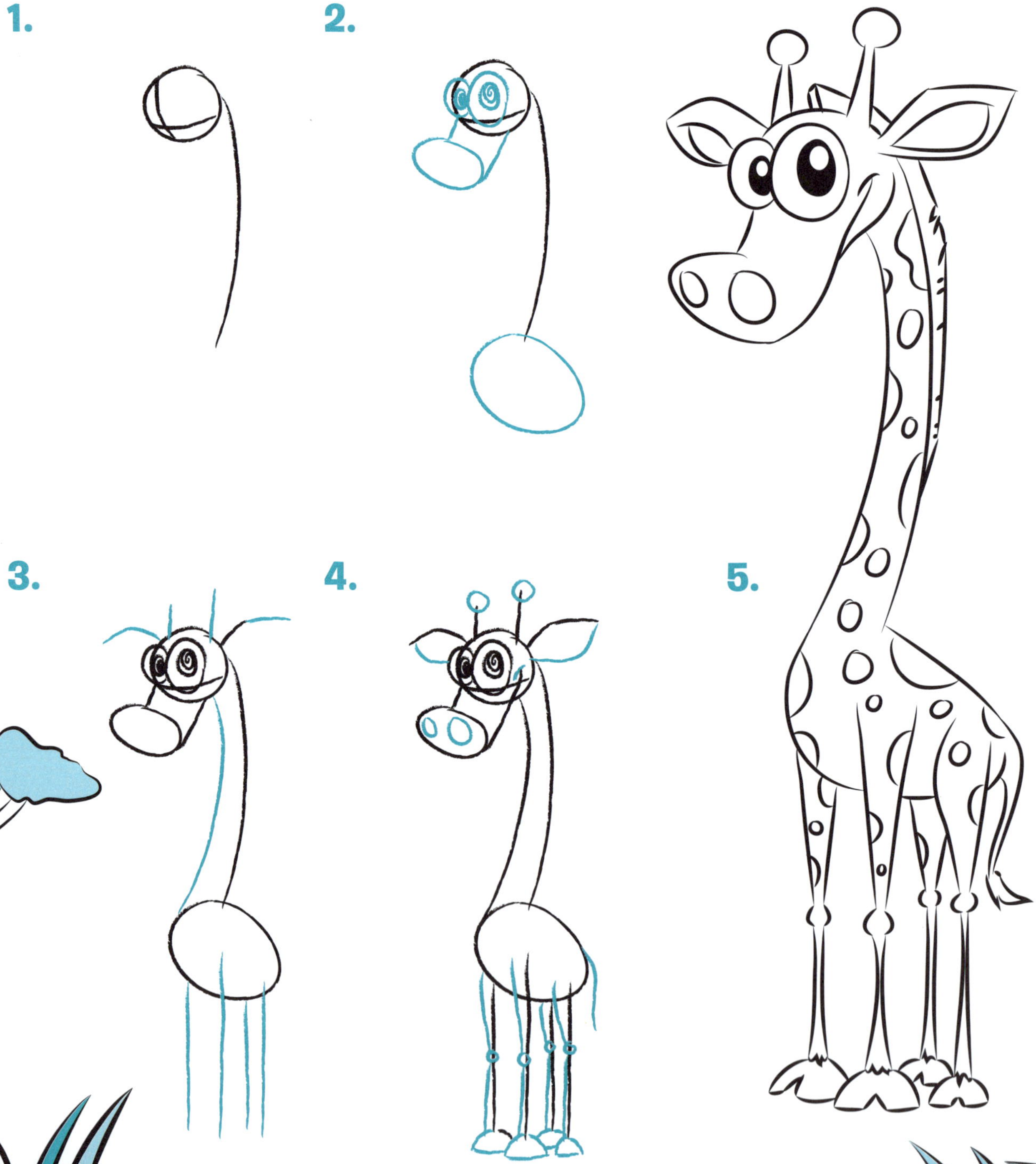

NOW IT'S YOUR TURN:

DID YOU KNOW?

A giraffe's legs are so long that it takes steps of up to 4.5 metres in length. It also sleeps standing upright.

MEERKAT

HOW TO DRAW A MEERKAT

1.

2.

3.

4.

5.

NOW IT'S YOUR TURN:

DID YOU KNOW?

This curious little mammal lives in a large family called a mob – sometimes with more than 50 members!

WARTHOG

HOW TO DRAW A WARTHOG

1.

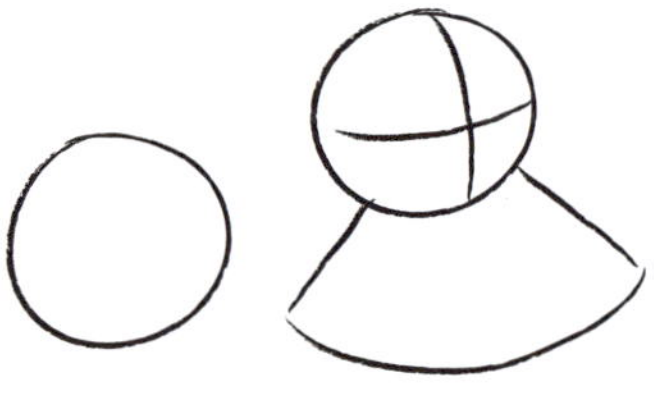

2.

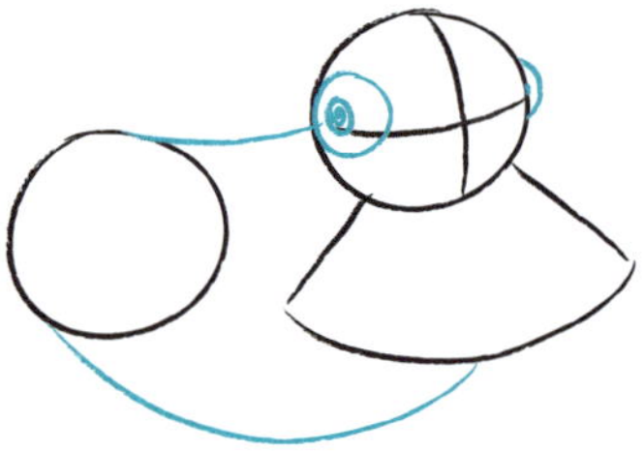

3.

4.

5.

NOW IT'S YOUR TURN:

DID YOU KNOW?

Warthogs get their name from bumps on their faces that look like warts. These wild pigs are mostly bald, although they do sport a luxurious mane of hair like a horse's.

ZEBRA

HOW TO DRAW A ZEBRA

1.

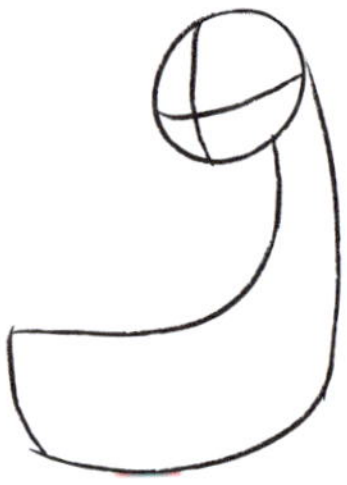

2.

3.

4.

5.

NOW IT'S YOUR TURN:

DID YOU KNOW?

Did you know that no two zebras' stripes are alike? Their stripes are unique to each individual, just like human fingerprints.

RECIPE

STRIPY ZEBRA CUPCAKES

MAKES 12 ZEBRAS

INGREDIENTS

250g / 1 cup sugar

4 eggs

250ml / 1 cup vegetable oil

250ml / 1 cup milk

1 tsp vanilla essence

300g / 2 cups flour

1 tbsp baking powder

2 tbsp cocoa powder

12-hole muffin tin with paper cases

ASK FOR YOUR PARENTS' HELP WITH: THE OVEN

1. Mix the sugar and eggs in a large bowl until light and frothy. Stir in the oil, milk and vanilla essence and mix well.
2. Combine the flour and baking powder. Gradually add the flour mixture to the large bowl and stir until you have a liquid batter.
3. Divide the batter into 2 equal portions. Stir the cocoa powder into one of the portions. You now have a yellow and a brown batter.
4. Preheat the oven to 180°C / 350°F.
5. Scoop a tablespoon of the yellow batter into each paper case. It'll slowly spread to the side of the case – this is good! Now add a spoonful of brown batter and let it spread again. Repeat until you have scooped 5 spoonfuls into each paper case.
6. Place the muffin tin into the oven and bake the cupcakes for 15–20 minutes until risen and brown. Remove from the oven and leave to cool, and then bite into one to uncover the zebra stripes on the inside!

TIP: If you want more stripes, add teaspoonfuls of batter rather than tablespoons.

RAINFOREST

GORILLA

HOW TO DRAW A GORILLA

1.

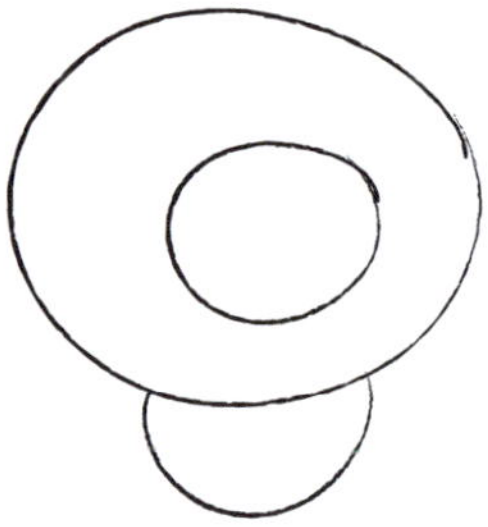

2.

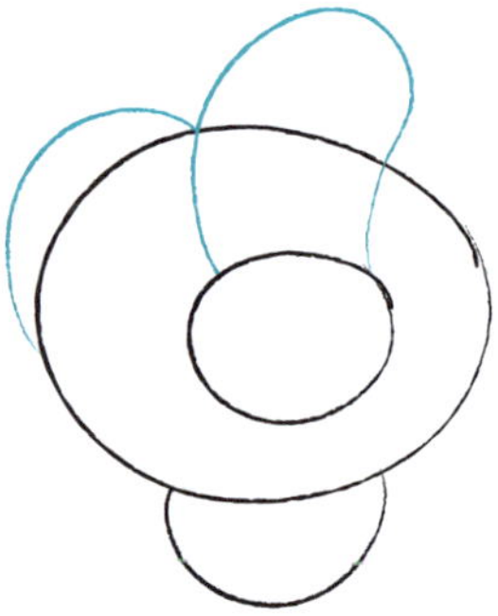

3.

4.

5.

NOW IT'S YOUR TURN:

DID YOU KNOW?

Gorillas are humans' closest living relatives, after the chimpanzees. Amazingly, we share around 98% of our DNA with these large primates.

RING-TAILED LEMUR

HOW TO DRAW A RING-TAILED LEMUR

1.

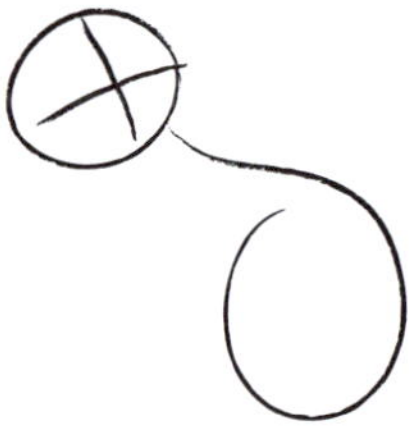

2.

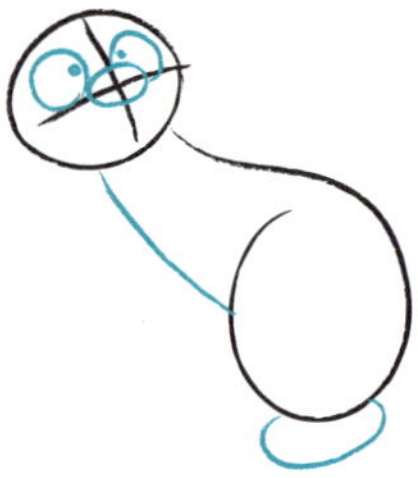

3.

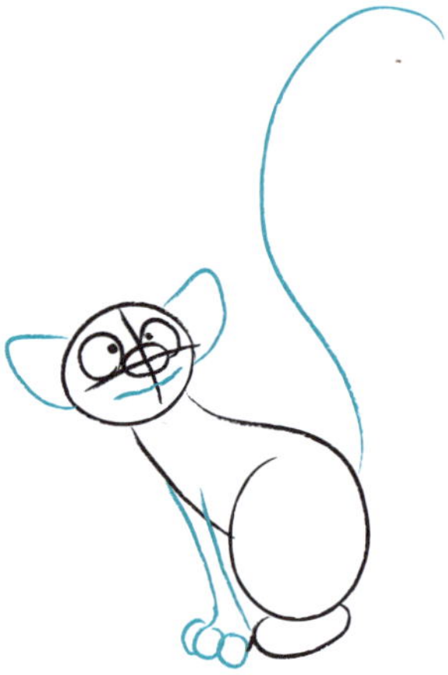

4.

5.

NOW IT'S YOUR TURN:

DID YOU KNOW?

These endangered animals can't grip with their tails like some of their primate cousins do. Instead, they use their hands and feet to move nimbly through the trees.

FROG

HOW TO DRAW A FROG

1.

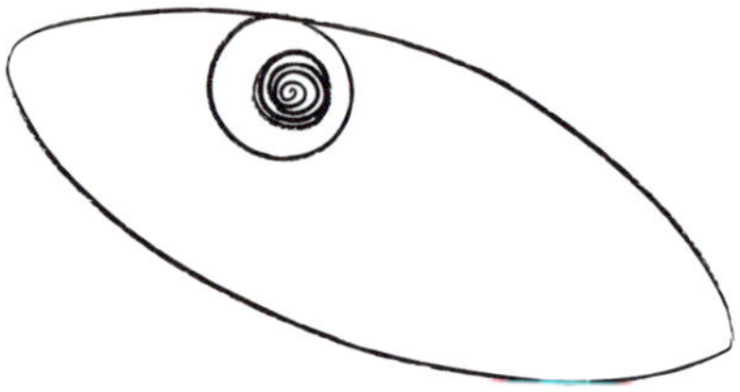

2.

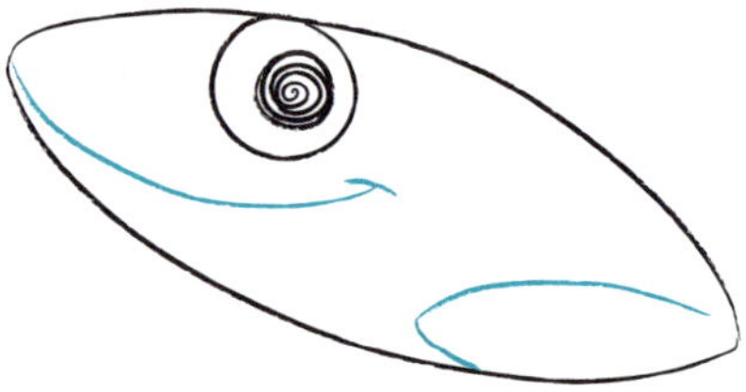

3.

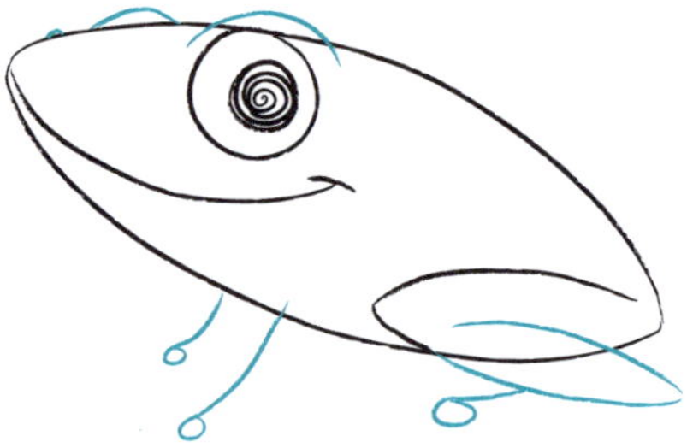

4.

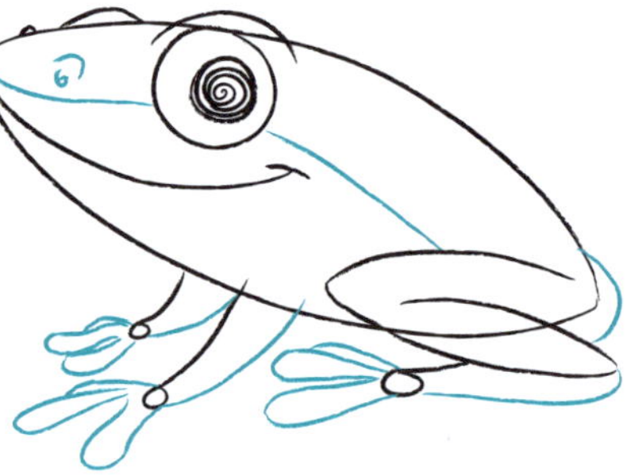

5.

NOW IT'S YOUR TURN:

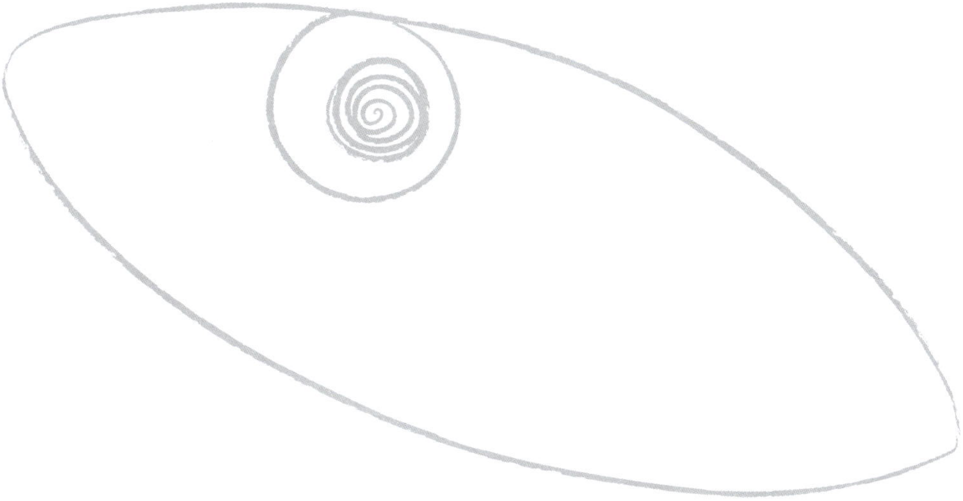

DID YOU KNOW?

To catch an insect, a frog throws out its sticky tongue, then snaps it back and swallows the insect.

BEAR

HOW TO DRAW A BEAR

1.

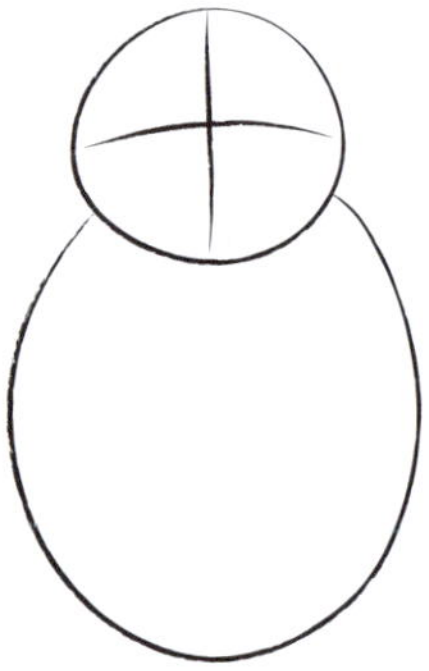

2.

3.

4.

5.

NOW IT'S YOUR TURN:

DID YOU KNOW?

Most bears have the ability to hibernate, which means they sleep through winter. Hibernating bears make their dens in burrows, caves, hollowed-out trees and rock crevices.

CHAMELEON

HOW TO DRAW A CHAMELEON

1.

2.

3.

4.

5.

NOW IT'S YOUR TURN:

DID YOU KNOW?

Chameleons can change their skin to blend in with surroundings. And did you know that their tongues are up to twice as long as their bodies?

BAT

HOW TO DRAW A BAT

1.

2.

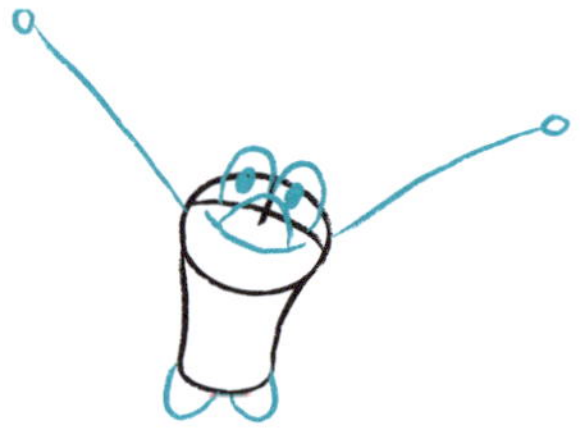

3.

4.

5.

NOW IT'S YOUR TURN:

DID YOU KNOW?

There are over 1000 different species of these flying nocturnal mammals. They feed on insects, fruit, fish and even blood!

RECIPE

GREAT GREEN FROG

MAKES 4 FROGS

INGREDIENTS

1 green apple
(like a Granny Smith)

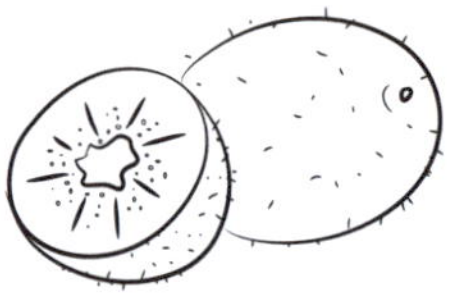

½ kiwifruit

Handful of white grapes

4 marshmallows

8 raisins

ASK FOR YOUR PARENTS' HELP WITH:
USING A KNIFE

1. Quarter and core the apple. Use a sharp knife to cut a long, thin mouth through the skin of each quarter. Place the frogs' faces on small plates.

2. Peel and slice the kiwifruit and cut each slice into quarters.

3. Halve the grapes – these will be your frogs' feet. Use scissors or a sharp knife to cut out little toes.

4. Place the kiwifruit and grapes on to the plate to make the frogs' legs and feet.

5. Cut the marshmallows in half and place them, sticky side down, on top of the frogs' faces.

6. Stick a raisin to each frog's eye to make pupils. The eyes should be sticky enough, but if not, use a little water or jam to glue them together.

OUTBACK

KANGAROO

HOW TO DRAW A KANGAROO

1.

2.

3.

4.

5.

NOW IT'S YOUR TURN:

DID YOU KNOW?

The largest living kangaroo, the red kangaroo, is also the largest living marsupial. Males can grow up to 1.8 metres in height and weigh up to 84 kilograms.

WOMBAT

HOW TO DRAW A WOMBAT

1.

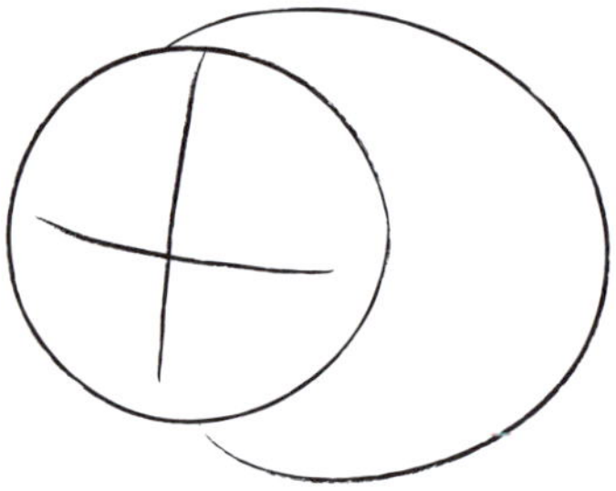

2.

3.

4.

5.

NOW IT'S YOUR TURN:

DID YOU KNOW?

Wombats love digging tunnels. They have a backward-facing pouch that doesn't fill up with dirt when they dig, which keeps their little joeys clean.

PLATYPUS

HOW TO DRAW A PLATYPUS

1.

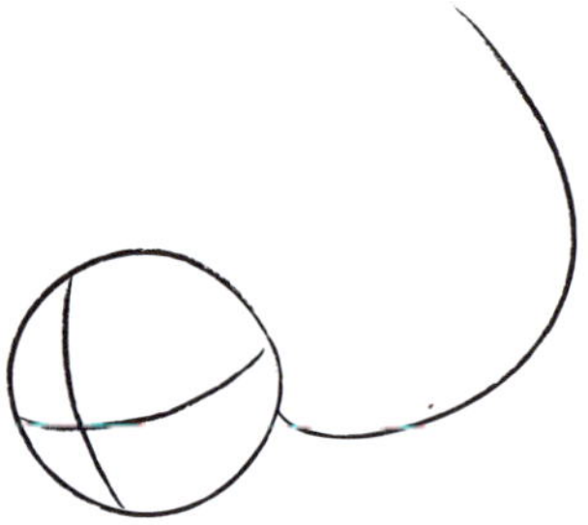

2.

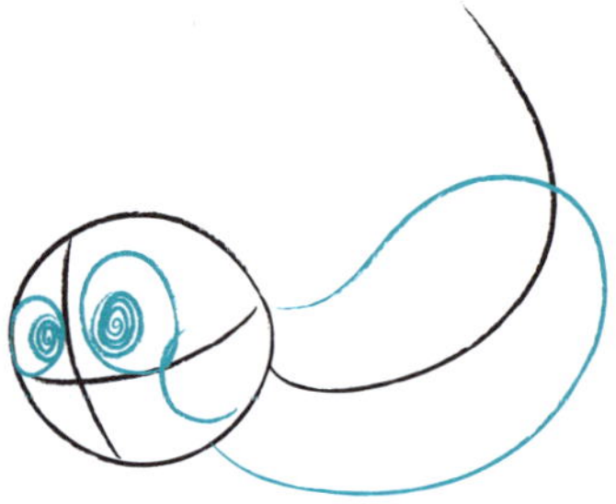

3.

4.

5.

NOW IT'S YOUR TURN:

DID YOU KNOW?

Platypuses don't eat underwater. They store their food in their cheeks and bring it to the surface to eat.

DINGO

HOW TO DRAW A DINGO

1.

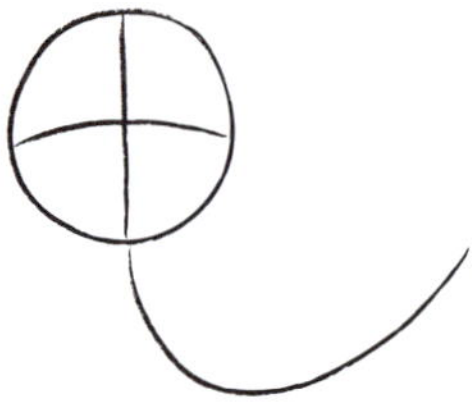

2.

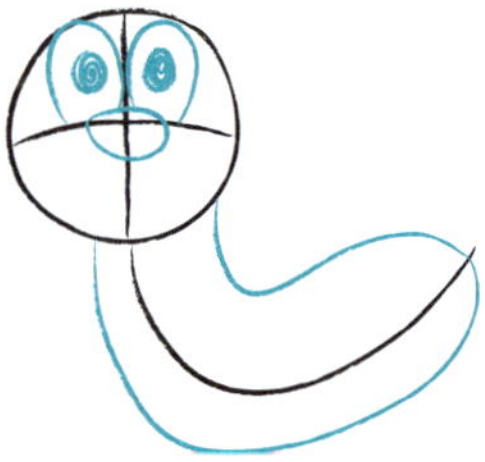

3.

4.

5.

NOW IT'S YOUR TURN:

DID YOU KNOW?

These wild dogs can live alone or in packs of up to 10 animals. They roam great distances and communicate with wolf-like howls rather than barking.

KOALA

HOW TO DRAW A KOALA

1.

2.

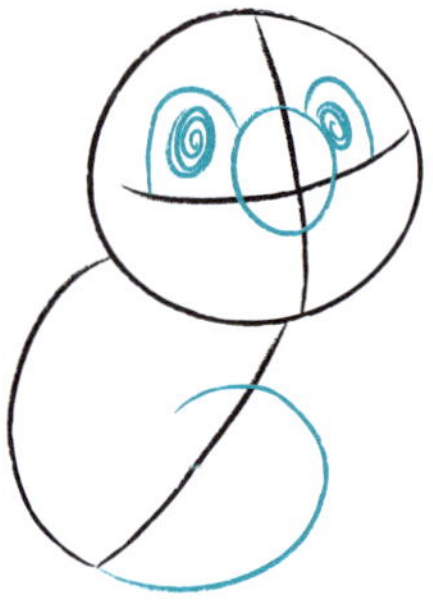

3.

4.

5.

NOW IT'S YOUR TURN:

DID YOU KNOW?

Koalas feed mostly on eucalyptus leaves, which are toxic for most other animals. They spend most of their time sleeping because digesting their toxic, fibrous, low-nutrition diet takes a lot of energy.

RECIPE

COOL KOALA COOKIES

MAKES 12 KOALAS

INGREDIENTS

125g / ½ cup soft butter

70g / ⅓ cup sugar

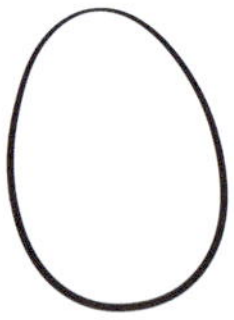

1 egg yolk

1 tsp vanilla essence

150g / 1 cup plain flour

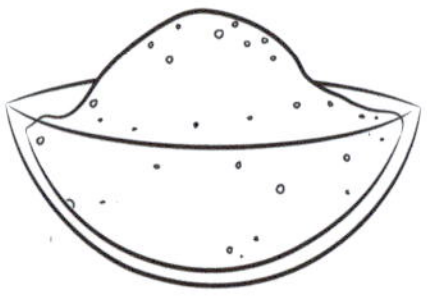

1 tsp cocoa powder

ASK FOR YOUR PARENTS' HELP WITH:
SEPARATING THE EGG YOLK, THE OVEN AND USING A KNIFE

1. Beat the butter and the sugar with a wooden spoon until the mixture is fluffy and light.

2. Mix in the egg yolk and the vanilla essence. Now add the flour bit by bit and keep stirring. It's hard work! Use your hands if the stirring gets too difficult.

3. Take a bit of dough the size of a walnut and put into a bowl. Add the cocoa and mash together to make the brown dough for the nose and eyes.

4. Divide the rest of the dough into 4 pieces and roll them into fat sausages. Then stick them and the brown dough in the fridge for 20 minutes to firm up.

5. Preheat the oven to 180°C / 350°F.

6. Cut each of the 4 dough pieces into 3 discs and place on a baking sheet lined with greaseproof paper. Press down on each cookie with a mug to flatten.

7. Shape little noses and eyes from the brown dough. Make dents with your thumb into the cookies, right where the nose and eyes should be. Gently push the nose and eyes into the dents.

8. Bake your koala cookies in the oven for 12–15 minutes until pale brown. Leave them to cool on a wire rack before eating.

TIP: You can also draw the nose and eyes onto the cookies after baking using a food pen with edible ink.

MARINE

SEAL

HOW TO DRAW A SEAL

1.

2.

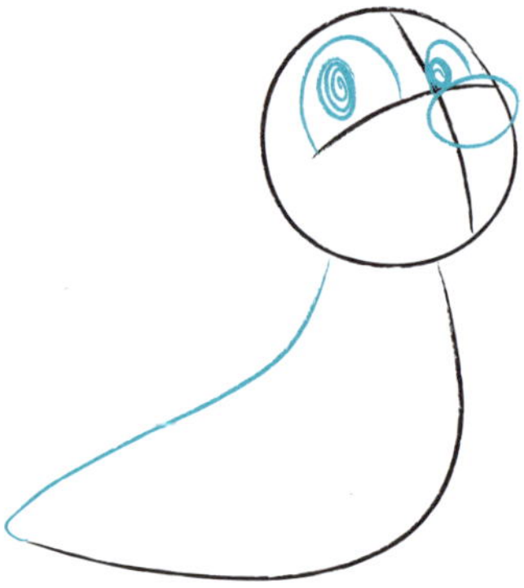

3.

4.

5.

NOW IT'S YOUR TURN:

DID YOU KNOW?

Some species of seal can spend up to two hours underwater before coming up for air.

WHALE

HOW TO DRAW A WHALE

1.

2.

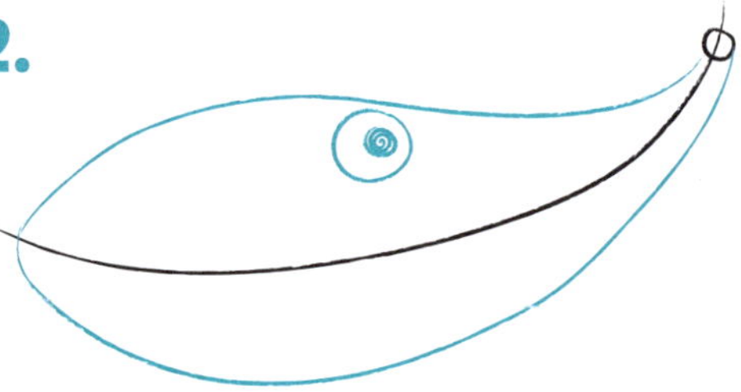

3.

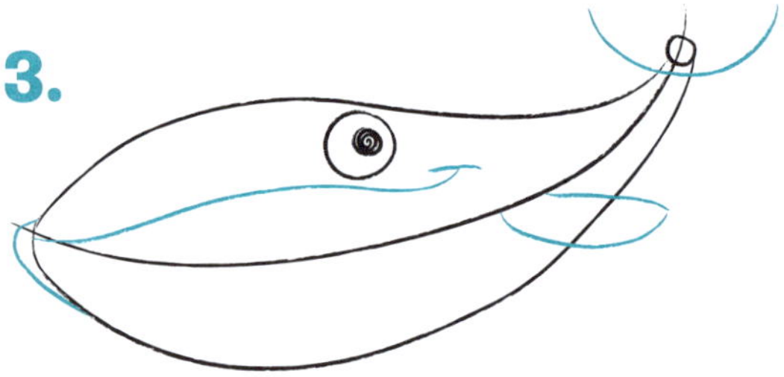

4.

5.

NOW IT'S YOUR TURN:

DID YOU KNOW?

Whales are actually mammals and need to surface for air, which they breathe in and out through a blowhole on their back.

PIRANHA

HOW TO DRAW A PIRANHA

1.

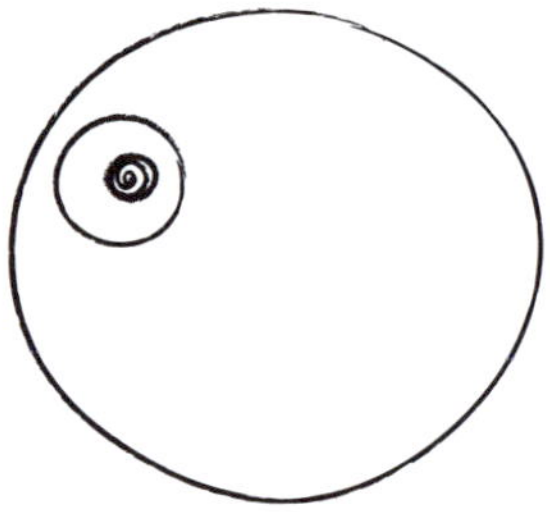

2.

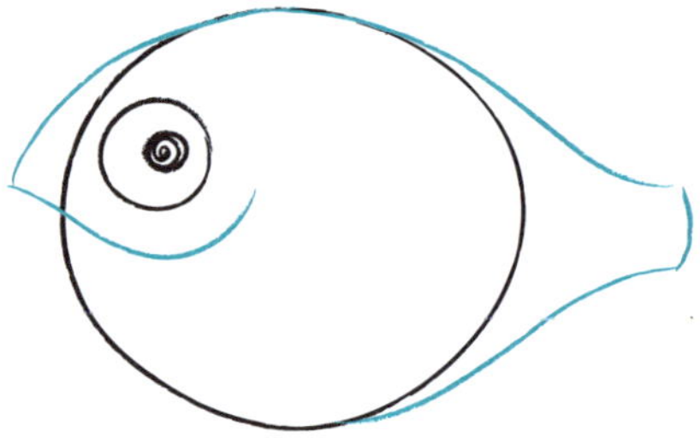

3.

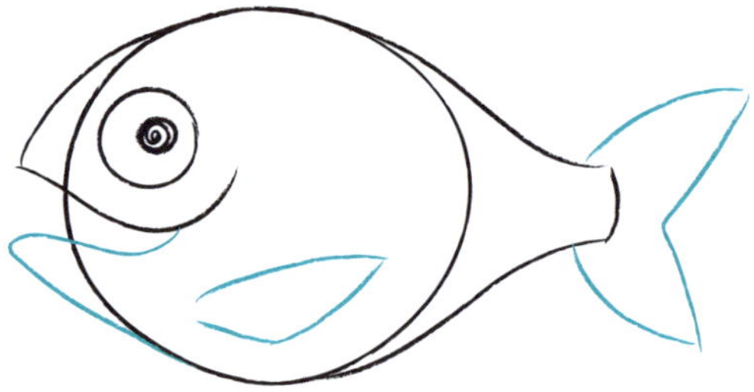

4.

5.

NOW IT'S YOUR TURN:

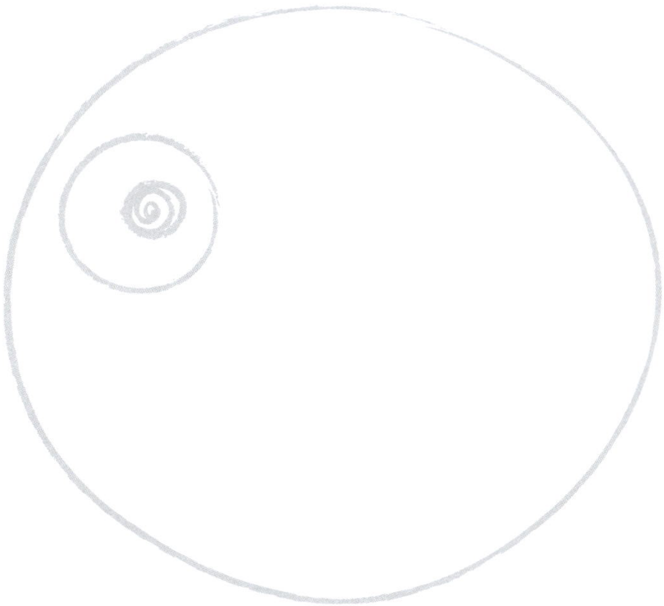

DID YOU KNOW?

Known for their sharp, pointy teeth, these fierce little freshwater fish have an insatiable appetite for meat and flesh.

CROCODILE

HOW TO DRAW A CROCODILE

1.

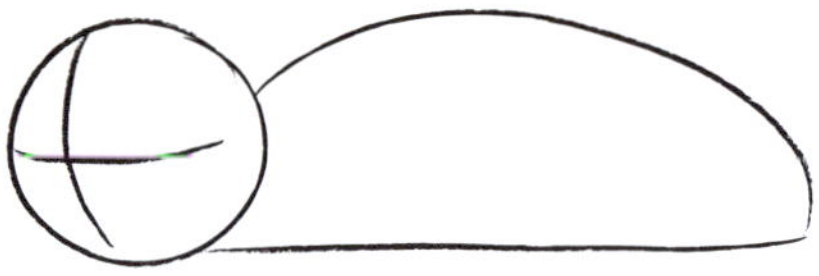

2.

3.

4.

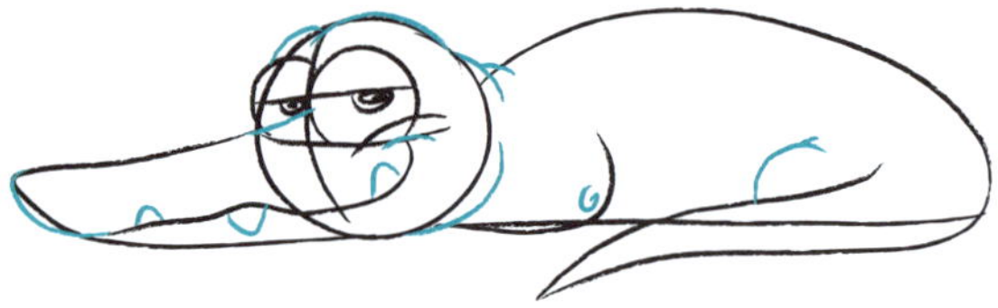

5.

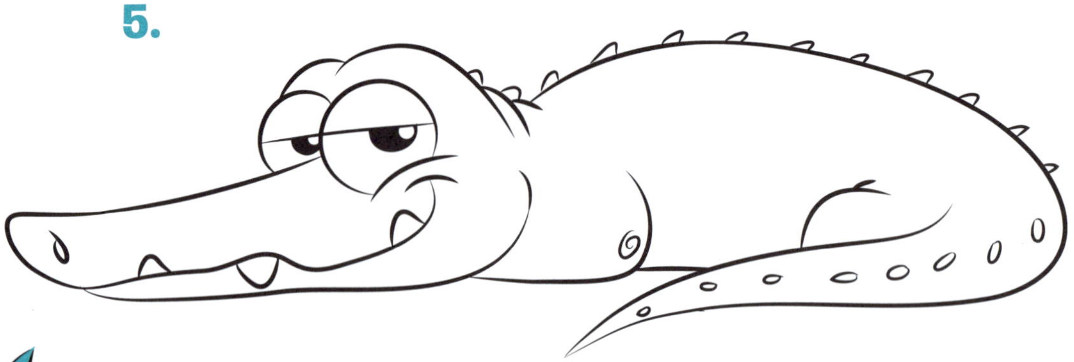

NOW IT'S YOUR TURN:

DID YOU KNOW?

These cold-blooded reptiles have a large set of sharp teeth and the strongest bite of any animal in the world.

TURTLE

HOW TO DRAW A TURTLE

1.

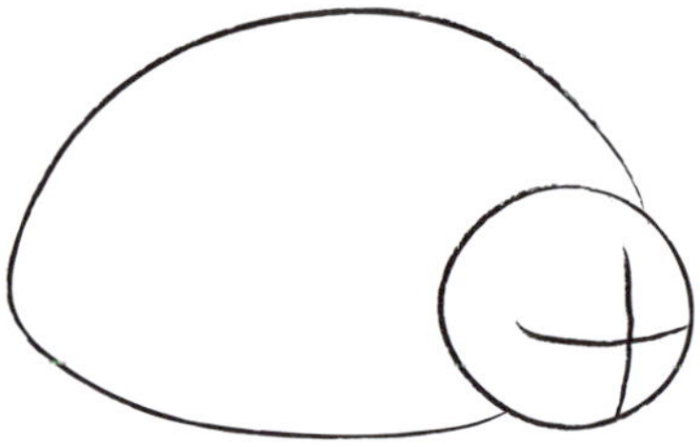

2.

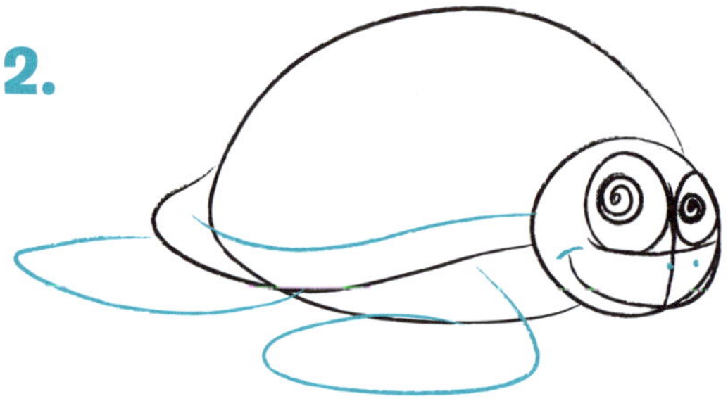

3.

4.

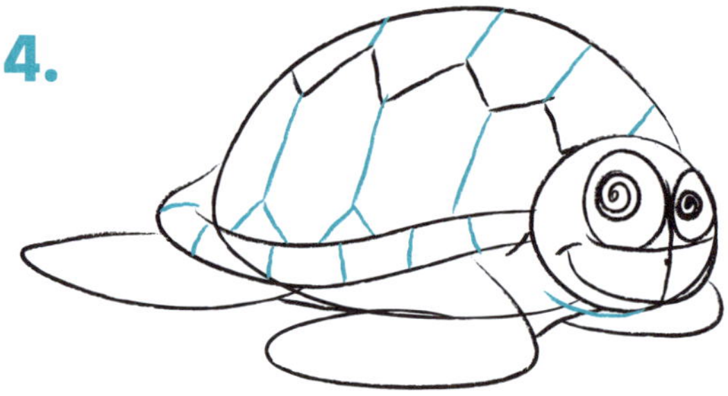

5.

NOW IT'S YOUR TURN:

DID YOU KNOW?

These funny-looking reptiles, with their wrinkly bald heads and protective shells, have been on the earth for more than 200 million years.

PENGUIN

HOW TO DRAW A PENGUIN

1.

2.

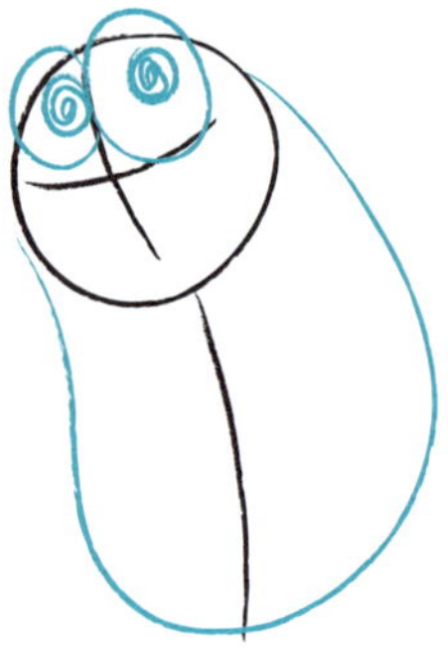

3.

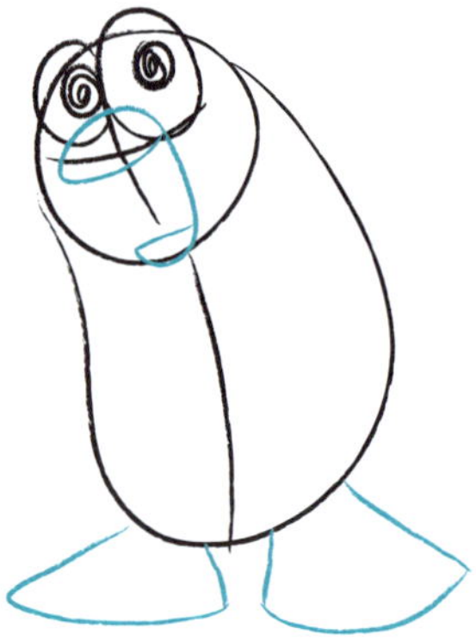

4.

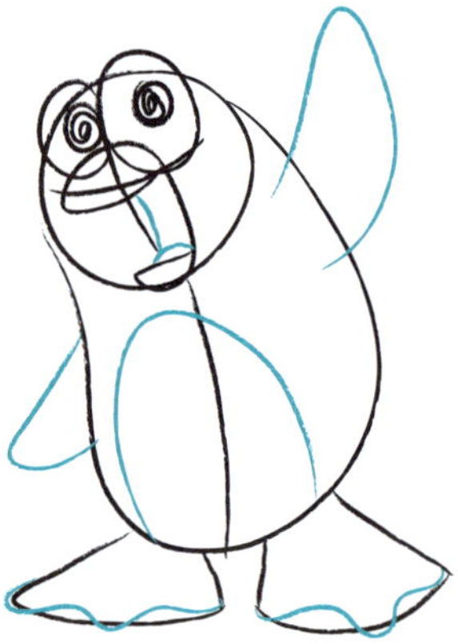

5.

NOW IT'S YOUR TURN:

DID YOU KNOW?

Penguins can't breathe underwater, but they can hold their breath for a very long time. They also drink salt water!

RECIPE

CUTE TURTLE ROLLS

MAKES 4 TURTLES

INGREDIENTS

100g
soft butter

1 tbsp
sugar

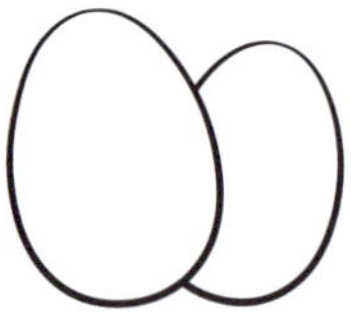

2 eggs

250g strong
white flour
(for bread)

½ tbsp
dry yeast

½ tsp
salt

100ml / 5 tbsp
milk

ASK FOR YOUR PARENTS' HELP WITH: THE OVEN

THE NIGHT BEFORE:

1. Mix the butter, sugar and eggs in a large bowl. It doesn't matter if it's a bit lumpy.

2. Add the flour, yeast, salt and milk. Stir with a wooden spoon or mix with your hands until you have a sticky dough. Cover the bowl with a damp tea towel and leave in the fridge overnight.

THE NEXT DAY:

3. Preheat the oven to 190°C / 375°F.

4. Divide the dough into 4 pieces. Take 1 piece, tear off a lump for the head and feet, and put to one side. Shape the big bit into a ball – this is the turtle's body. Use the small lump to shape 5 more balls: a head and four small feet. Stick these to the turtle's body using a tiny bit of water as glue. Do the same for the other 3 pieces of dough.

5. Place the turtles on a non-stick baking sheet. Bake in the oven for 20 minutes until they're golden brown.

TIP: You can use a wooden skewer to draw a crisscross pattern on the turtle's back. It'll look even more real!

BIRD SANCTUARY

FLAMINGO

HOW TO DRAW A FLAMINGO

1.

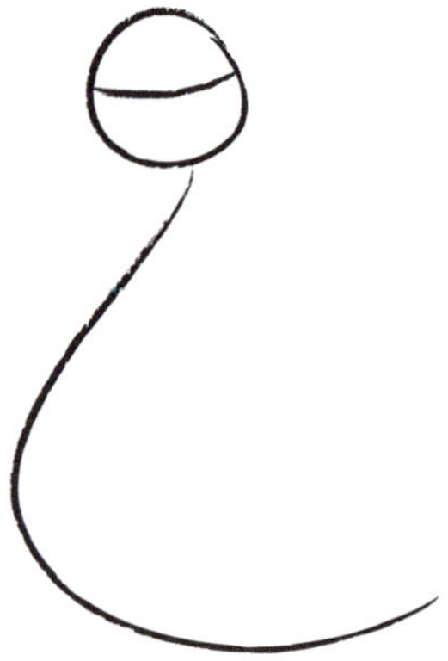

2.

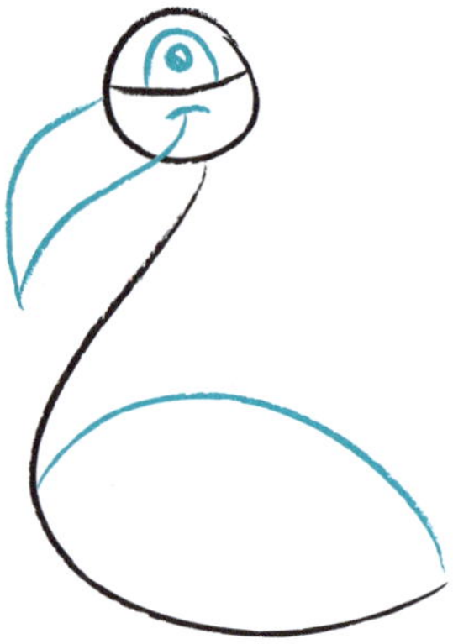

3.

4.

5.

NOW IT'S YOUR TURN:

DID YOU KNOW?

Flamingos are born grey or white. It takes them up to three years to develop their fabulous pink, orange or red plumage.

VULTURE

HOW TO DRAW A VULTURE

1.

2.

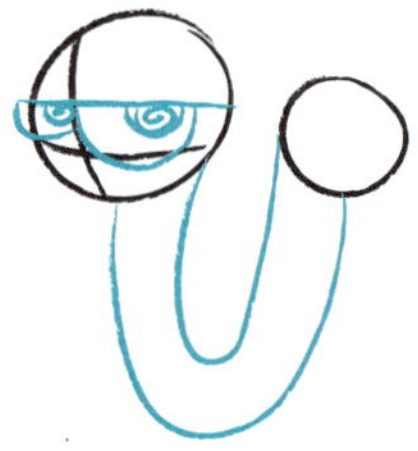

3.

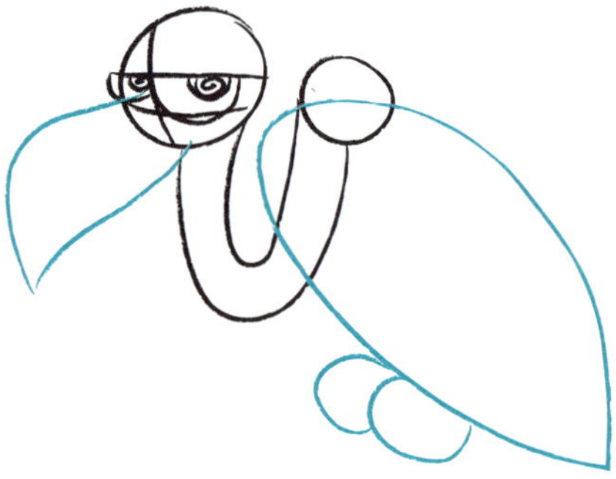

4.

5.

NOW IT'S YOUR TURN:

DID YOU KNOW?

A group of vultures is called a **committee**, **venue** or **volt**. In flight, a flock of vultures is a **kettle**.

TOUCAN

HOW TO DRAW A TOUCAN

1.

2.

3.

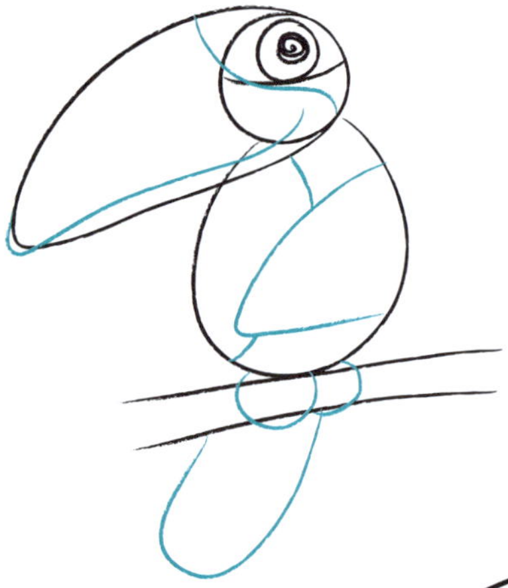

4.

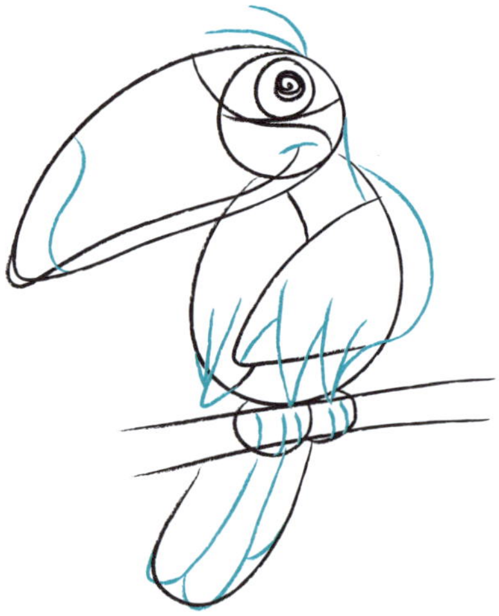

5.

NOW IT'S YOUR TURN:

DID YOU KNOW?

Adult toucans are known for their oversized, colourful beaks, but they aren't born that way. A baby toucan is born with a tiny beak, which grows bigger as the toucan grows bigger!

PEACOCK

HOW TO DRAW A PEACOCK

1.

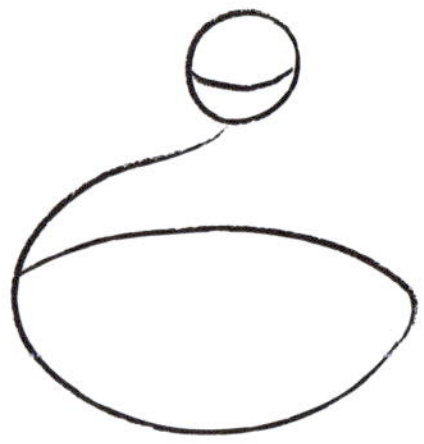

2.

3.

4.

5.

NOW IT'S YOUR TURN:

DID YOU KNOW?

Male peafowl are called **peacocks** and female peafowl are **peahens.** Babies are **peachicks.** Only peacocks have vibrant blue-green plumage and extravagant tail feathers.

OWL

HOW TO DRAW AN OWL

1.

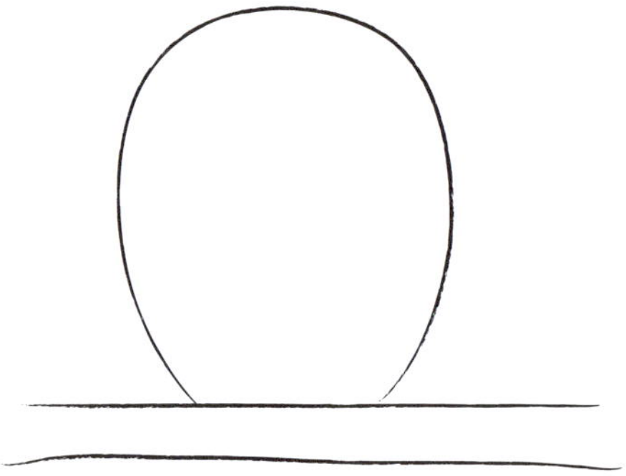

2.

3.

4.

5.

NOW IT'S YOUR TURN:

DID YOU KNOW?

These birds of prey have three eyelids: one for blinking, one for sleeping and one for keeping the eye clean and healthy.

RECIPE

GOOD OWL PIZZA

MAKES 2 OWLS
(ENOUGH FOR 4 CHILDREN, OR 2 VERY HUNGRY ONES)

INGREDIENTS

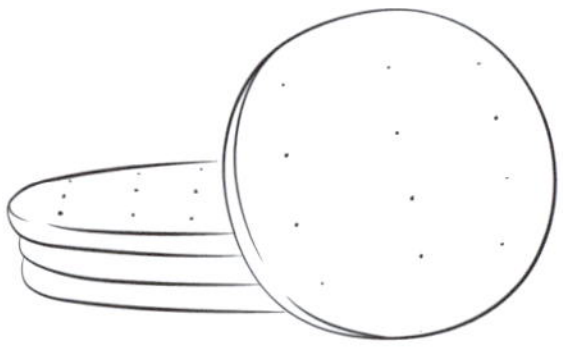

4 mini ready-made pizza bases or pita-breads

4 tbsp tomato puree

Handful of grated Parmesan cheese

1 large tomato

¼ yellow capsicum

½ zucchini

Handful of olives

Slice of carrot or piece of Parmesan cheese

ASK FOR YOUR PARENTS' HELP WITH:
THE OVEN AND USING A KNIFE

1. Preheat the oven to 220°C / 425°F.
2. Spread the tomato puree over the pizza bases and sprinkle with the grated Parmesan.
3. Cut the tomato into thick slices and use the nicest ones for the owls' eyes.
4. Cut the capsicum into strips and place them onto the pizza to make the owls' wings.
5. Slice the zucchini and cut each disc into quarters. Use these to make the feather belly.
6. Cut the olives into slices and use these to finish the eyes and make little toes.
7. Finally, cut a triangle out of the carrot or Parmesan and place under the owls' eyes to make little beaks.
8. Bake the owl pizzas in the oven for about 7 minutes.

SERVE HOT!

CREEPY CRAWLIES

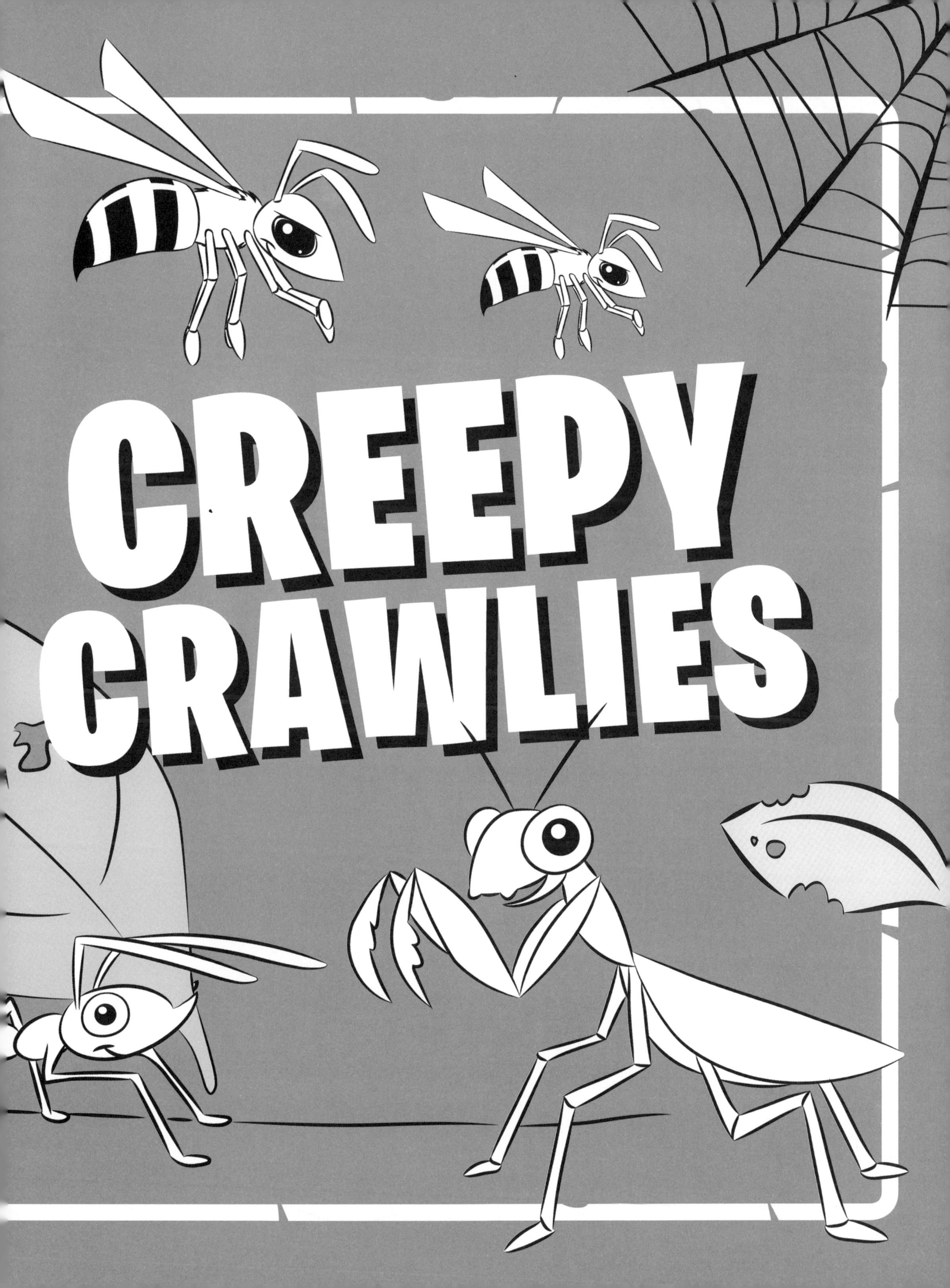

SPIDER

HOW TO DRAW A SPIDER

1.

2.

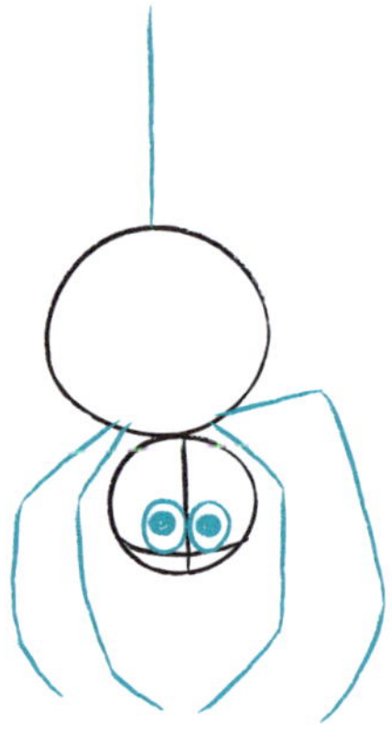

3.

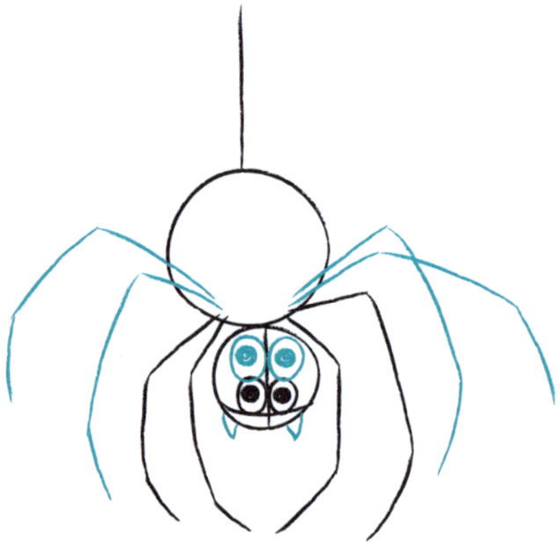

4.

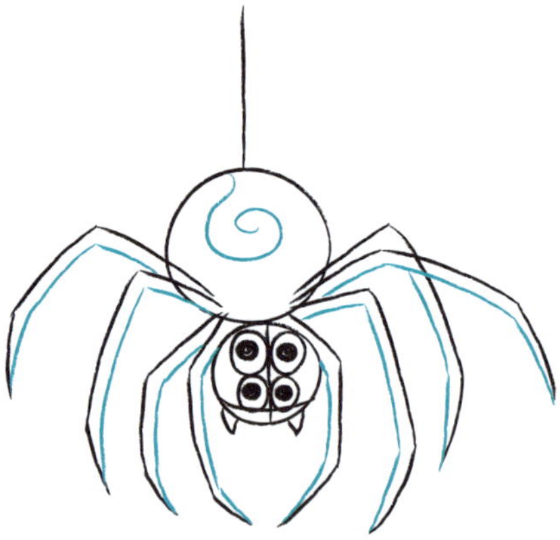

5.

NOW IT'S YOUR TURN:

DID YOU KNOW?

Spiders are arachnids, not insects. They also have 4 eyes. Scarily, female spiders will eat male spiders if they're hungry!

LEAFCUTTER ANT

HOW TO DRAW A LEAFCUTTER ANT

1.

2.

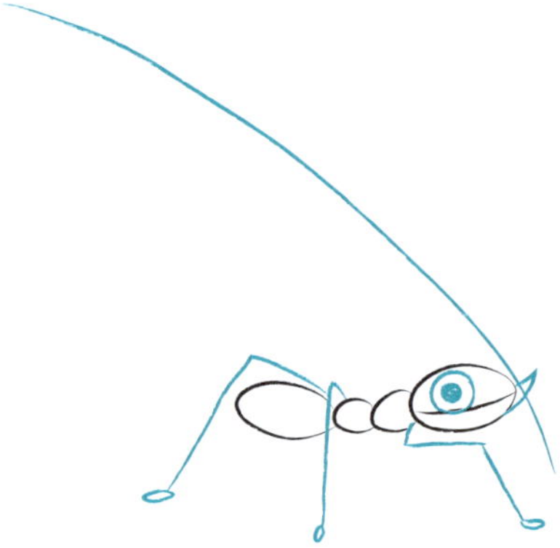

3.

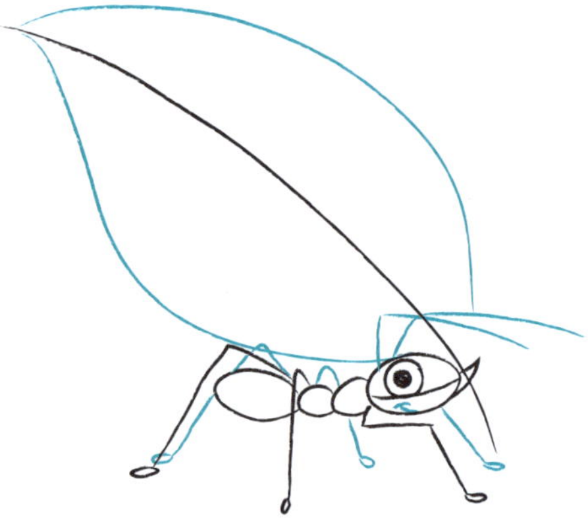

4.

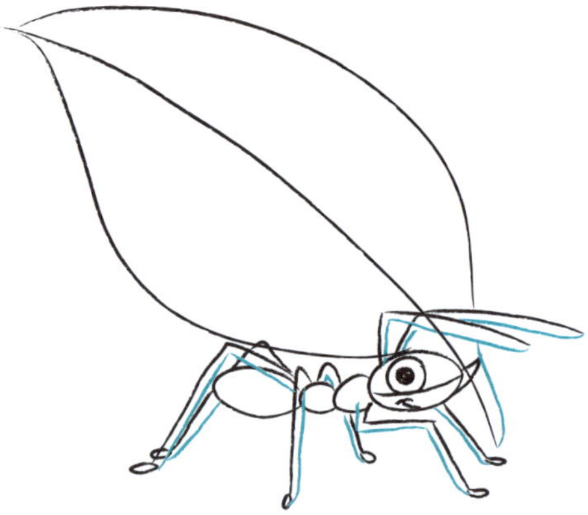

5.

NOW IT'S YOUR TURN:

DID YOU KNOW?

These little ants can carry up to 50 times their own body weight. This is like a 10-year-old kid carrying a giraffe!

PRAYING MANTIS

HOW TO DRAW A PRAYING MANTIS

1.

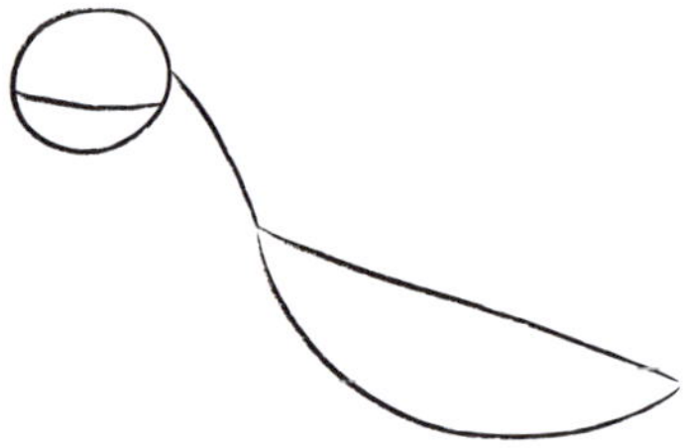

2.

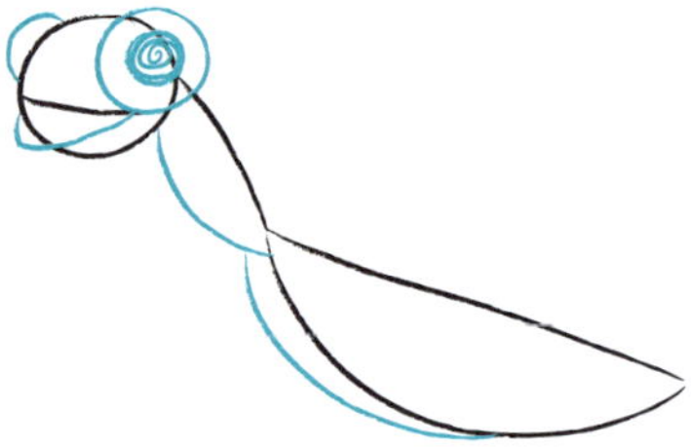

3.

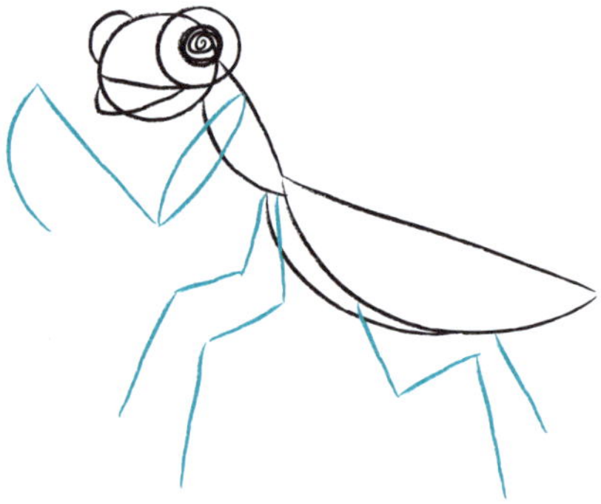

4.

5.

NOW IT'S YOUR TURN:

DID YOU KNOW?

These carnivorous insects get their name from their prayer-like pose.

WASP

HOW TO DRAW A WASP

1.

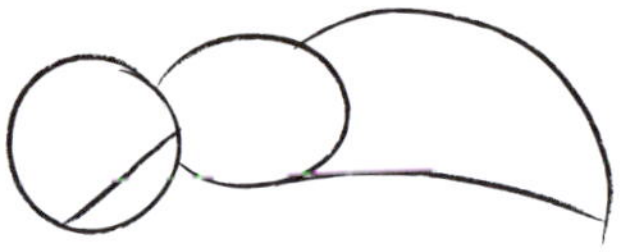

2.

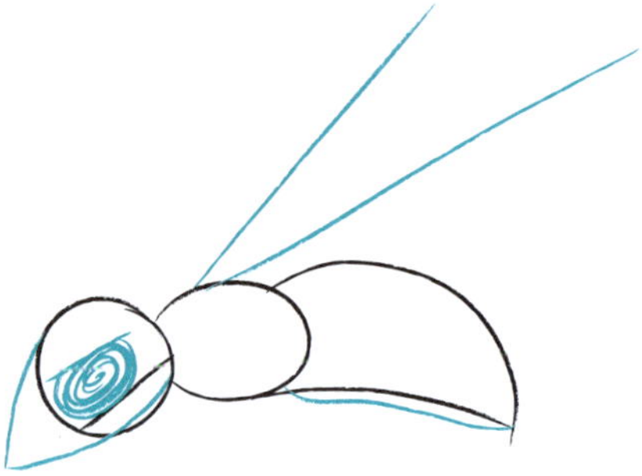

3.

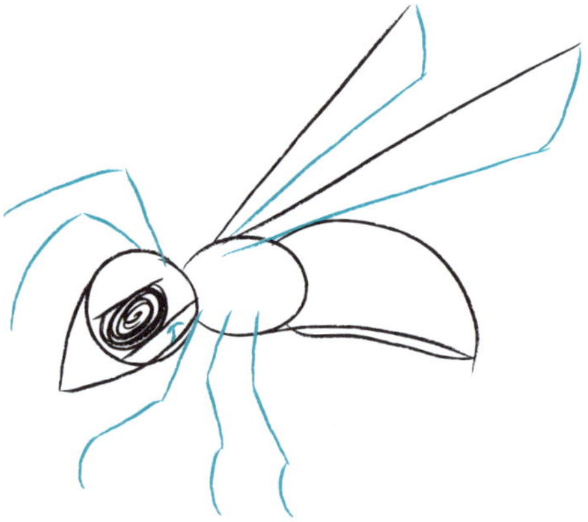

4.

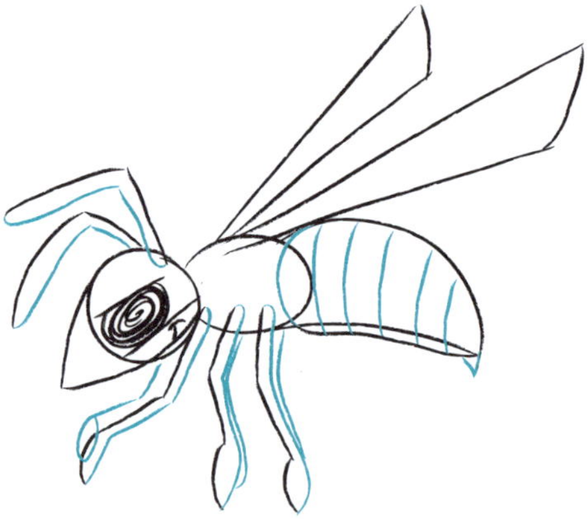

5.

NOW IT'S YOUR TURN:

DID YOU KNOW?

Wasps are known for their poisonous sting. Unlike bees, they can sting repeatedly.

SCORPION

HOW TO DRAW A SCORPION

1.

2.

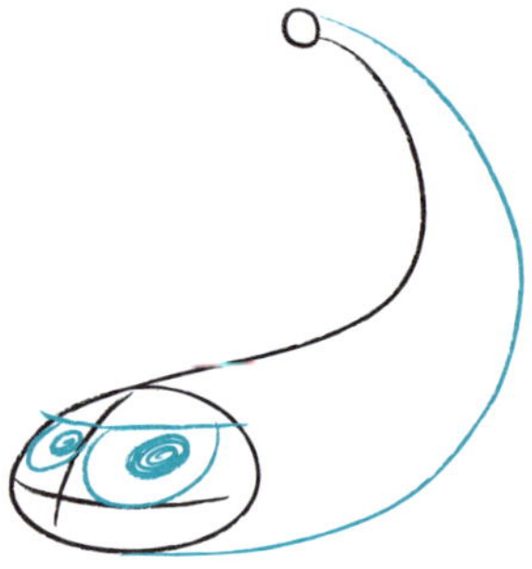

3.

4.

5.

NOW IT'S YOUR TURN:

DID YOU KNOW?

These arthropods have a pair of large grasping claws and a segmented tail with a venomous stinger on the end.

RECIPE

SCARY SPIDER PIES

MAKES 4 SPIDERS

INGREDIENTS

1 apple

125g / 1 cup mixed berries (frozen)

2 tbsp sugar

Pinch of cinnamon

Knob of butter

1 sheet puff pastry (frozen)

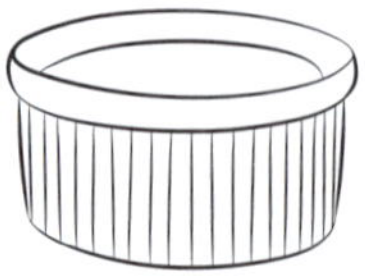

4 ramekins, each 100 ml / ½ cup

ASK FOR YOUR PARENTS' HELP WITH:
THE OVEN AND USING A KNIFE

1. Preheat the oven to 200°C / 400°F.

2. Peel and core the apple. Cut into little chunks and mix them in a bowl with the berries, sugar and cinnamon. Keep 8 small berries to one side.

3. Defrost the puff pastry and use the upside down empty ramekins to cut out 4 circles. These are your spider bodies.

4. Cut the rest of the dough into strips that are as long as your ramekins are high. You'll use them as the legs for your spiders.

5. Rub the insides of the ramekins with butter. Fill them with the fruit mixture.

6. Stick 6 legs to each spider body, using a little water as glue.

7. Carefully drape a pastry spider over each ramekin. Push down on the legs a bit so they stick to the sides of the ramekin.

8. Bake the spider pies for 20–25 minutes until golden brown. Remove from the oven and leave to cool a little, then stick two eyes (berries) on top of each pie and serve.

TIP: Lovely with custard!

WELL DONE,
MY LITTLE APPRENTICES.

Now you can draw the whole zoo - and cook some yummy treats too!